Color Donald Trump

Love him or hate him, now you can color him.

Ponzi Madoff

ISBN-13:
978-1543173130

ISBN-10:
1543173136

www.ingramcontent.com/pod-product-compliance
Lightning Source LLC
Chambersburg PA
CBHW062146280526
45788CB00001B/329
9781543173130